THE STORY OF

Mosses, Ferns and Mushrooms

Photographs by MYRON EHRENBERG

THE STORY OF

MOSSES, FERNS

AND

MUSHROOMS

by DOROTHY STERLING

DOUBLEDAY & COMPANY, INC. • GARDEN CITY, NEW YORK

ACKNOWLEDGEMENTS: The authors would like to express their gratitude to Dr. Donald P. Rogers of the New York Botanical Garden and to Dr. Ralph C. Benedict, President of the American Fern Society, for their careful reading of the manuscript and examination of the photographs.

We would also like to thank the American Museum of Natural History for permitting us to photograph a fossil fern; Knaust Brothers, Inc., of Coxsackie, N. Y., for permission to take pictures in one of their mushroom caves; and Mr. and Mrs. Sterling Parker, Pleasant Valley, Conn., for assisting us in taking many of the fern pictures; and to Mr. Charles Mohr and Mr. Bradley of the Audubon Nature Center, Greenwich, Connecticut for their helpfulness in locating some of the ferns and mosses.

The drawings on page 17 are reproduced by courtesy of the Brooklyn Botanic Garden, the photograph on page 74 by courtesy of the U.S. Department of Agriculture.

Library of Congress Catalog Card Number 55-7012

Books by Dorothy Sterling
with photographs by Myron Ehrenberg

Contents

THE STORY OF

Mosses, Ferns and Mushrooms

CHAPTER ONE

The Time-Machine

When you were little, the world seemed a simple place. There were big people and little people, good things and bad. When you cried, the big people comforted you. When you smiled, they smiled too. Very simple.

But the older you get, the more complicated life becomes. You learn one thing today and something quite different tomorrow. Take spelling, for instance. In second grade you were taught to spell "new." N-E-W. By third grade there was another word, pronounced the same way, only you spelled it K-N-E-W. In fourth grade it was G-N-U. And when you study French, you spell it N-O-U-S.

Crazy? Contradictory? No. *New* is spelled correctly. So is *knew* and *gnu* and *nous*. The first facts you learned aren't wrong. They are only a part of the story. The older you get, the more parts you learn. It's like a jigsaw puzzle. You need to put all the pieces in their proper place in order to see the whole picture.

This book is about plants. Do you know what a plant is?

"Of course," you answer. "It grows in the earth. It has roots and a stem. And flowers and fruit and seeds."

Anything else?

"It's small like a daisy and big like an oak tree," you add. "And it's green."

A very good answer. But you might also have said, "Plants grow on rocks and in the water. They have no roots and stems, no flowers and fruit. Instead of seeds, they have spores. Many of them are smaller than daisies. Some aren't green at all."

Crazy? Contradictory? No. Both answers are correct. They are both pieces of the whole picture.

A daisy is a plant and so is an oak tree. But a moss is a plant and so is a fern and a bright orange mushroom. Instead of flowers and seeds, these plants have spore cases and spores. They live and grow in a different way from daisies or oak trees. Just as you live differently from a frog or an elephant, even though all three of you are animals.

These differences go back to the way life on earth began. Daisies weren't always blooming in the fields, nor were there oak trees in the woods—or boys and girls to climb them.

Two billion years ago

Let's imagine that you could hop into a time machine and fly backward for two billion years or so. The earth—our earth —would look very strange.

As far as you can see, there are rocks and water, water and rocks. The only sound is the breaking of the waves along the shore. The only movement is caused by the wind and the rain. The only colors are the gray-brown rocks and the deep blue sea. No grass on land, no fish in the water.

But just wait. The first living things are forming in the sea. They start as jellylike, colorless, single cells. As you watch, something new is added. You notice it first in the shallow pools of water at the edge of the sea. At low tide, you see it on the rocks. A new color. The green of plant life.

Here is a big change. The thing that makes plants green is a chemical known as *chlorophyll*. With the help of chlorophyll,

ROCKS AND WATER

plants can manufacture their own food. When the sun shines, green plants combine water and air to make sugar. This sugar is the basic food for animals as well as plants.

The clock in your time machine ticks off a million years and another million years. One-celled plants have grown into two cells, two into four. Colonies of cells clump together or form long narrow ribbons. Some fasten themselves to the ocean bottom with little suckers. Animals swim through the water

BRANCHING SEAWEEDS

with the help of tiny hairs. Now you can recognize branching seaweeds and jellyfish and sponges.

When storm winds blow, the waves tear some of the seaweeds from their moorings and toss them high up on the rocks. High and dry. The plants shrivel in the sunlight. They cannot make food without water. They die.

The rocks turn green

A million years go by and another million. Plants are slowly climbing from the tidal pools at the oceanside and learning to live along the rocky shore. These are not the long, branching seaweeds, but tiny dots of green. They lie flat, hugging the

PIONEERING PLANTS: LIVERWORTS

bare, damp rocks, drinking in water with all parts of their bodies.

Gradually these pioneering plants experiment and change. They grow rootlike threads which anchor them to the rocks. They become two cells thick, and three, with the upper layer of cells acting as a protective skin, so that the precious water will not evaporate.

Their success brings other changes. You have watched the waves pounding on the shore, breaking off bits of rock and grinding it into fine sand. You have seen the wind blowing the sand and the rain washing it into the sea. Now these grains catch in the living and dead bodies of the plants. They form soil, and the soil becomes a storage tank for water. The rocks are no longer bare.

A million years go by and another million. A few bold plants are trying new experiments. Instead of lying flat, they grow upright. The rootlike threads which served at first only as anchors can now drink up water and minerals from the earth. Frail stalks, only an inch or two high, carry this water to tiny leaves.

Once this works, so many other experiments take place that you can't keep up with them all. There are plants with underground stems and no roots. There are plants with woody, forking stems and no leaves. There are plants with needle-thin leaves and others with broad, thick leaves. There are plants which have no chlorophyll and must get their food ready-made from their green neighbors.

The quiet forest

The time-machine clock slowly ticks away. Seven hundred million years have passed since you first looked for life in the sea. The rocks are green and a thousand different kinds of

16

TWO BILLION YEARS AGO

plants flourish in the warm, moist atmosphere. There are lush forests even in the far north, with trees a hundred feet tall.

But the forests are strangely different from the woods you know today. No birds sing. No squirrels chatter. No bees or

ANCIENT FOREST

17

ANCIENT TREES: HORSETAILS

ANCIENT TREES: GROUND PINE

butterflies flap their wings. Occasionally a giant dragonfly zooms overhead or a salamanderlike creature pokes his snout through the mud of the swamp.

Even the trees are odd-looking. Some have jointed green trunks with frills of leaves growing at each joint. Some have narrow leaves covering both trunk and branches. Some have scaly bark, patterned like alligator hide. Other trees look like ferns, but these ferns are fifty feet tall with woody trunks and leaves six feet long.

The earth is green, but it is only green. There are no pink flowers in the spring, no yellow or brown fruits dangling from branches in the fall, no flaming autumn colors. There are no seeds for birds to eat, no nuts for squirrels to store, no blossoms where bees may hunt for nectar. You are in a forest of flowerless plants.

As you hover around in the time machine, the earth's crust shrinks and stretches. Mountains rise. Valleys form. The swampy forests are drowned in a sea of mud. The tall trees topple over and die. Then rocks and sand wash down from the mountains and new forests grow. A million years, ten million years, fifty million. Again and again the process is repeated. There are sandwiches of plants and mud, plants and mud, which are slowly squeezed into coal.

Fossils, dead and living

Most of the plants inside the mud sandwiches decay and disappear. A few leave their imprint on the layers of coal or are hardened into rock. These are the fossils that tell the story of ancient plants. The fossil print in the photograph on the next page shows the leaf of a fern, a fern that lived more than three hundred million years ago—before the dinosaur, before the mammoth and the saber-toothed tiger, and long, long before you and I.

Put on your jacket and close the windows of the time machine. There's a cold wind blowing. A great icecap, forming at the South Pole, is spreading over South America and most of Africa. In the Northern Hemisphere the inland seas are drying up and the swamps slowly turn into deserts. The climate of the earth is changing and plants and animals must change too.

Some of the forest trees disappear entirely. Others shrink in size until they are dwarf copies of their former giant selves. Still others survive by trying out something new—flowers and seeds. Until now, all plants have reproduced themselves by spores. In a dozen different ways, seed plants have a better chance of living in extremes of heat and cold, in dry places as well as wet, on mountains and deserts and level plains.

FOSSIL FERN

With the time machine speeding toward modern times, the landscape becomes more and more familiar. There are giant reptiles browsing in pine forests. The last of the dinosaurs crashes through an underbrush of dogwood and willow and poplar. You find oak trees in the woods and daisies in the meadow long before you see men struggling to stand upright.

The time machine swoops down for a landing as the hands of its clock point to today. Has the two-billion-year nonstop flight gone too quickly? Would you like to go back to some of the local stations? Sprawl on the rocks to examine the first land plants? Slosh through the swampy coal forests? Cover your hands with bright-colored spores and solve the mystery of the plants which cannot make their own food?

You don't need a time machine to carry you backward. Of all of the different kinds of plants known today, nearly half are living fossils—plants that grow almost the way the first plants on earth grew, millions of years ago. These are the liverworts and mosses and lichens, the mushrooms and horsetails and ferns.

The ancient world of flowerless plants still exists all around you. You have only to go outdoors to find it.

CHAPTER TWO

Meet the "Firsts"

Now it's time for a few introductions. The first "firsts" of all, the green plants you saw forming in the sea, are *algae* (singular, *alga*). Some algae are so small that you can't see them without a microscope. Others grow to enormous size. There are kelps in the Pacific Ocean reported to be six hundred feet long. They hold the title of World's Largest Plants.

The seaweeds you find at the beach are algae. So is the green scum on the surface of ponds and the bright green slime on wet rocks. "The old oaken bucket, the moss-covered bucket" in the song is probably covered with algae, not moss. The algae that grow on rocks and on old buckets look like splashes of green paint. You can't pick an alga as you would a flower. You have to scrape some off with your fingernail.

Algae haven't changed much in a billion years. They are still water plants. Even the big seaweeds that can take the beating of the waves and the pull of tides have no protection against dry air. They can live only in water.

A giant step

The honor of being the first land plant is usually awarded to the *liverwort*. Each liverwort plant is only an inch or two long

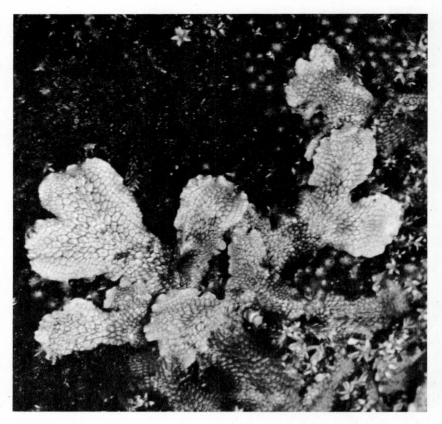

LIVERWORTS

and scarcely thicker than a sheet of paper. It wouldn't look like much alongside a kelp. But the liverwort has taken a giant step from water to land.

A liverwort is made up of several layers of cells, each with its own job to do. The topmost layer acts as a skin, to prevent evaporation of water. Food is manufactured in the middle layer, while from the lower surface grow the hair-thin threads that anchor the plant in place. The plants creep over the rocks, forking and reforking. As they grow from the tip, they die at the base, so that they never become very long.

Despite the improvements in body plan which make life on land possible, liverworts are not really free from their watery past. You will find them in damp, shady places in the woods or alongside streams. The liverworts in the photograph grow beside a waterfall. Only a few feet away, out of range of the spray from the splashing water, there is no sign of them.

Perhaps you are wondering about the liverwort's odd name. Men studied this tiny plant long before the days of liverwurst sandwiches on rye bread. Because its rounded lobes reminded them of the shape of the human liver, they named it liverwort (*wort* means plant). They even thought it would cure diseases of the liver!

Heads up!

Not all liverworts are liver-shaped. Some, with creeping stems and tiny leaves, are often mistaken for their cousins, the *mosses*. The ancestors of the mosses were those bold adventurers who first tried growing upright instead of hugging the rocky shore. They didn't get very far with their experiments. Few mosses are more than six inches tall. But they took another big first step.

There are close to twenty thousand different kinds of mosses. And there are also dozens of plants that are called "moss" although they have no more than a nodding acquaintance with the moss adventurers. Irish Moss, which grows in the ocean off the shores of New England, is a seaweed. Reindeer Moss, which covers the ground in the Maine woods, is a lichen. (You will meet the lichens in Chapter 3.) Spanish Moss, which hangs from the branches of live oaks in Florida and South Carolina, is a flowering plant. So is Moss Pink, which forms bright clumps in rock gardens each spring.

CARPET OF MOSS

FERN MOSS

MNIUM MOSS

Almost any low-growing green plant is likely to be called moss. "A green carpet on the forest floor" is the way the poets describe it. Pretty, but rather dull. Not much to be said about it.

Actually there is a great deal to be said about mosses. If you examine the "green carpet" you will see that it is made up of hundreds of separate plants. Some mosses resemble miniature ferns or tiny feathers. Others look like green flowers or palm trees or pines. There are mosses only one quarter of an inch high and others more than a foot above ground. There are white mosses and brown mosses and some that are wine-red.

Mosses are tough as well as pretty. They live all year round at the Arctic Circle, hibernating in the long winter months under blankets of ice and snow. They live in tropical forests at the equator and on the rocky slopes of Mount Everest. They grow in swamps and on city pavements. The only place you won't find them is on the desert.

These little plants wouldn't be able to live in all sorts of climates if they hadn't learned a few tricks. They need water to make food. They also need some kind of protection for the grains of chlorophyll, which dry up in the bright sunlight. They cannot store water in their roots or trunk the way an oak tree can. Their leaves are thin and delicate, not thick and waterproof the way a daisy's are. How do you suppose they solve the problem of summer sun and drought?

They solve it by giving in to the weather. They stop making food. They stop growing. Instead of holding their leaves

HAIRY-CAP MOSS IN DRY WEATHER

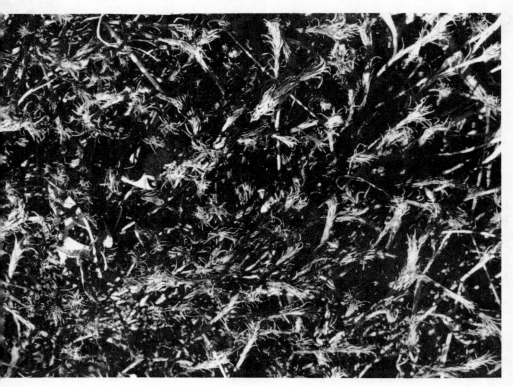

toward the sun, they fold them or curl them up. This cuts down on evaporation of water and protects the delicate chlorophyll grains. Because the green coloring matter is hidden, the plants look brown or white or gray.

Compare the photographs on this and the opposite page. Both show a clump of Hairy-cap Moss. But the first picture was taken during a dry spell in midsummer. The leaves are folded and brown, the stems twisted. The plants look dead, but they aren't. If you pour a glass of water on them, you will see some action. They will wriggle and uncurl like a handful of worms. Soon they will be standing up straight, their brown leaves once again green.

HAIRY-CAP MOSS IN DAMP WEATHER

New mosses from old

Mosses can live through a hot summer or a winter of sub-zero temperatures, but they need moisture in order to produce new moss plants. In this respect they are more dependent on water than the flowering plants are. Remember, they are only two steps removed from their relatives in the sea.

Mosses grow from *spores*. A spore is a single cell, simple and primitive when compared with a seed. Every seed contains a baby plant and enough stored-up food for the baby to live on until it can manufacture its own. Spores are just tiny sparks of

MOSS SPORE CASES

life. They don't contain baby plants or food. Usually they form new plants *unlike* the plants on which they grew.

Before you throw up your hands and say that the-life-of-a-moss-is-hopelessly-complicated-and-you-don't-care-if-you-never-understand-it, perhaps you will have time to take a walk. In spring or early summer you are sure to see something unexpected.

There are wiry stems growing out of the green moss carpets, and each stem has a little bag on top. These bags are *spore cases*, containers for the ripening spores. Some are as round as balls. Others look like pipes or eggs or birds' beaks. Green when they first appear, they later become orange or brown or red.

The spore case in the close-up photographs on the next page

MOSS SPORE CASES

MOSS SPORE CASES

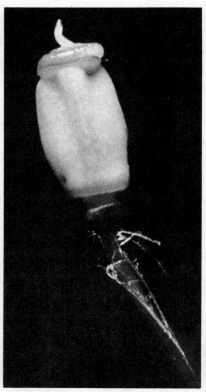

HAIRY-CAP MOSS SPORE CASE WITH AND WITHOUT CAP

belongs to the Hairy-cap Moss. If you pull off the hairy cap which gives the plant its name you will see that the case is shaped like a cylinder with a tight-fitting round lid. Both cap and lid fall off as the spores ripen. Then the sides of the case wrinkle and push out the spores.

If the spores land where there is enough moisture, they begin to grow. The baby moss is at first a mass of branching green threads, covering a square inch or two. It looks like one of its alga relatives. Soon buds appear on the threads, buds which produce tiny stalks and slender leaves.

32

When you look at the photograph on this page you can see that some of the new moss plants are topped by flowerlike cups. These are male plants, each producing hundreds of sperm cells. The plants with the narrow pointed leaves are females. Inside the overlapping leaves there are eggs.

When the sperms are ripe, they swim to the eggs and fertilize them. Notice the word *swim*. The corkscrew-shaped sperms are covered with fine hairs. They move through the water by wriggling these hairs, as if they were small sea animals. The water comes from raindrops or dew or melting snow.

HAIRY-CAP MOSS: MALE AND FEMALE PLANTS

Without water, there would be no swimming. Without swimming, there would be no fertilization. Without fertilization, there would be no new moss plants. Now you can see why mosses are more dependent on water than the flowering plants are.

The fertilized egg does not grow into a green, leafy moss. Instead it produces a wiry stem, topped by a plump spore case. This is really a new kind of plant, but because it is green for only a short time it cannot make its own food. It lives as a parasite, getting its food from the mother plant.

The male and female clusters of the Hairy-caps grow on separate stems. In many other mosses, both are found on one plant. No matter what the arrangement, however, all mosses have the same life history. Their way of reproducing themselves is called an *alternation of generations*. Another way of saying this is: parents and children never look alike; grandparents and grandchildren always do.

HAIRY-CAP MOSS: SPORE-BEARING PLANT

The green leafy parent produces a wiry-stemmed spore case. The spore-case parent produces a green leafy moss plant.

This complicated way of reproduction is only a part of the story. If something happens to interrupt it, or if there is no water for the sperms to swim in, mosses have other methods to fall back on. Otherwise they would never have been able to cover so much ground for so many millions of years.

Most mosses live on year after year, sending out new shoots in the spring from the tips of last year's plants. They also spread from underground branches. In dry places, some mosses never even attempt to form spores. They depend on the wind to carry away broken-off bits of leaves or branches from which new plants start.

You have probably read that crabs grow new claws if their old ones are destroyed. Mosses can do this too, only better. If you take a single moss leaf and put it in a dish of water, it will produce fine green threads in a few days. Then buds will appear on the threads, each one developing into a new plant. It's as though a claw could grow a new crab!

How do you do?

It is not always easy to meet the mosses. Some of them are so small and shy that you can be introduced to them only through a magnifying glass. Others can be recognized by the shape of their leaves or their nodding spore cases.

The Hairy-cap Moss seems like an old friend. It is both the most common moss and the largest in our part of the world. You will find patches of these plants, looking like little trees, wherever you walk—alongside the road, in the fields and woods. They tower over the other mosses, growing to a height of eighteen inches in cool, damp places. They are sometimes nicknamed "pigeon wheat" because their spore cases are the

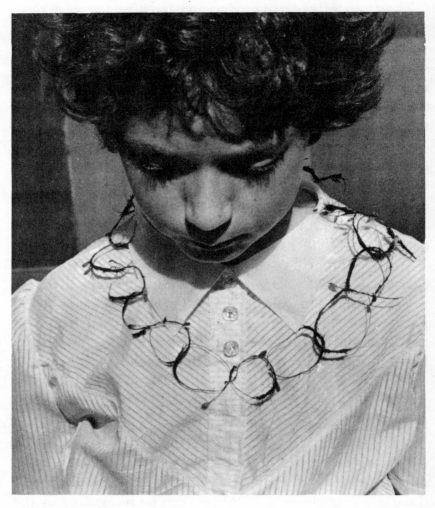

HAIRY-CAP MOSS NECKLACE

size of wheat grains. Children who live in the country often pick Hairy-cap plants and weave them into necklaces and bracelets.

If you turn back to page 26, you will meet the feathery Fern Moss. It creeps along the ground, or it covers the surface of a damp rock or tree stump. Its tiny leaves are scalelike and overlapping. Because they look like the needles on cedar trees, this moss is also called Cedar Moss.

Facing the Fern Moss on page 27 is the Mnium (pronounced ni′ um). Seldom more than two inches tall, this moss clusters at the base of trees and alongside streams. Its spore cases are cylinder-shaped and its bright green leaves make you think of flower petals.

Pincushion Moss plants crowd together to form rounded spongy cushions. In the woods these cushions may be two or three feet across. Soft and gray-green in damp weather, during dry spells they become white and crumbly. Their more sci-ientific name is White Moss.

PINCUSION MOSS

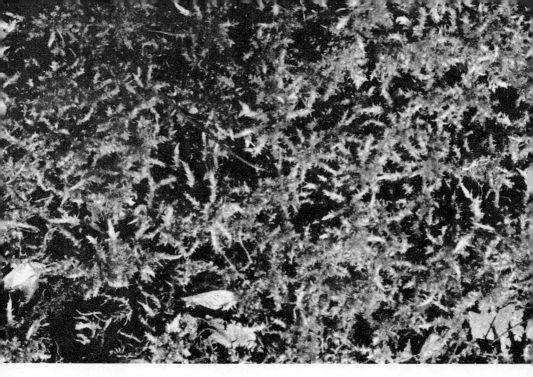

PEAT MOSS

The Peat Mosses have a special story of their own. You will meet them in swampy places. Often they grow in the water, forming a thick mat on the surface of a pond. As the older parts of the plants die, new ones continue to grow until there is a moss raft several feet thick.

By this time there isn't much left of the pond. The pond has turned into a bog. The mat of moss is strong enough to support your weight. It feels springy when you walk on it but you won't sink through to the water underneath. This kind of bog is known as a *quaking bog*.

The quaking bog continues to fill up with the dead bodies of swamp plants until there's no more pond at all. The pond has turned into land. It is filled with black spongy soil.

But that's not all. After a while the dead plant bodies which make up the land become so tightly pressed together that they can be cut into blocks. These dried blocks are used as fuel in many parts of the world. The land has turned into *peat*. It is on its way to becoming coal. Although most peat bogs are thousands of years old, the change from moss to peat can be accomplished in twenty-five years.

Peat Moss plants are pale and floppy-stemmed, with pointed glistening leaves. They grow to be several feet long. The cells in their leaves and stem are larger than those in other moss plants and are able to soak up enormous quantities of water. One plant can hold two hundred times its own weight in water.

SINGLE PEAT MOSS PLANT

If you don't believe this, try squeezing a handful of this moss to see how much water you can wring out. Because it is more absorbent than cotton, it is sometimes used for surgical dressings.

Another name for Peat Moss is Sphagnum (pronounced sfag'nm). Even if you have never seen it growing in a swamp, you have probably met it in one form or another.

Do you know a gardener? When he buys rose bushes or lilacs from a nursery ask him to save the greenish-white stuff in which the roots of the plant are wrapped. This is Peat Moss. It keeps the roots of the bush damp until the gardener has time to plant it.

Peat Moss is also sold by the bale, each bale being made up of thousands of dried and shredded plants. Gardeners dig the bits of moss into clay or sandy soil. When it rains, the dried plants swell up again and help the soil hold moisture.

CHAPTER THREE

A Dead-end Road

You have met the algae on the old oaken bucket and the liverworts clinging to the rocks. You have seen the mosses beginning to stand up straight. So far everything has moved ahead in an orderly fashion. One-two-three. From tiny one-celled plants to the beginnings of roots and leaves and stems.

Next you would expect to find plants with sturdier roots and broader leaves and longer, stronger stems. One-two-three-four. Each kind of plant becoming a little bigger and a little tougher until finally there is an oak tree. A gradual progress from little to big, from simple to complicated, from lower forms of life to higher forms.

The trouble is that history isn't always orderly. The history of plants can't be told just in a one-two-three-four succession. Neither can the history of animals or the history of man.

It's as if you were climbing a mountain. The road isn't a straight one. There are curves and bumps and detours. There are valleys and plateaus. When you come to a crossroad, you see two signs. One says, "This way to the top." The other says, "Dead-end road."

The inhabitants of the dead-end roads long ago stopped climbing the mountain. They will never lead the way toward bigger, sturdier plants. Some of them have even become smaller and weaker than they used to be. They are stick-in-the-

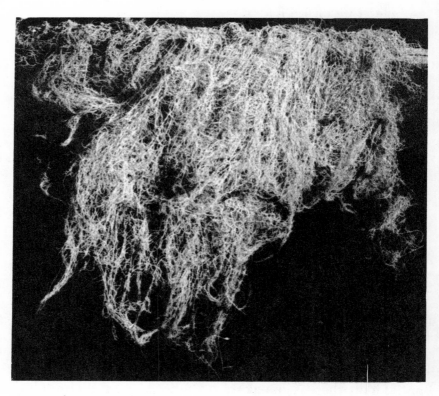

OLD MAN'S BEARD LICHEN

muds, so to speak. But they are a part of the plant jigsaw puzzle. You need their pieces in order to see the whole picture.

Lichens (pronounced li' kns) are plants that don't fit into a one-two-three-four history. Many lichens are flatter than liverworts. Some are taller than mosses. They grow on rocks and they hang from tree branches and they cover the ground in coral-shaped clusters. They have no leaves, no stems, no roots. For more than a billion years they have lived on a dead-end road.

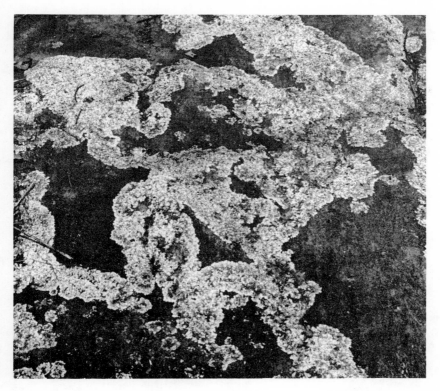

PARMELIA LICHEN

When men first began to study plants, they didn't know what to say about lichens. They thought that lichens grew out of the rocks, that they were, in a way, the children of the rocks. They thought the bare stone had given birth to living plants!

This wasn't just an idea of the cave men or the ancient Egyptians. It is what many people thought even a hundred years ago. It wasn't until 1866 that a scientist, looking into his microscope, solved the mystery of the lichens.

The flat pattern of green on the rocks is not one plant but a colony of plants. Hundreds of them. You can see some of these separate plants in the close-up picture. What you cannot see without a microscope, however, is that every member of the colony is not one plant but two. A lichen consists of a green alga surrounded by a colorless *fungus*.

Fungi (the plural of fungus) are plants without green coloring. They cannot make their own food. They must get it instead from other plants or animals. The fungi you are probably most familiar with are mushrooms. You will read more about them in the next chapter.

PARMELIA LICHEN, CLOSE-UP

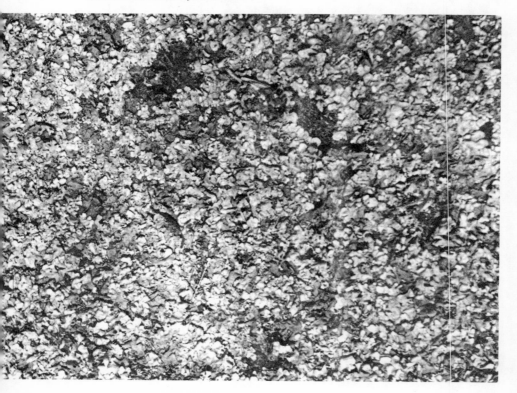

The algae and fungi that make up lichens have a very practical arrangement. The green algae make the food. The threads of the fungi wrap around the algae, protecting them from the hot sun, anchoring them to the rocks, and helping them find water. The two tiny plants are partners. Their partnership makes it possible for them to live together in places where one alone could never survive.

Plant scientists can "make" lichens in their laboratories. They grow algae and fungi in test tubes and then introduce them to each other. When the fungi curl around the algae, the plants are able to support themselves without further help from the scientists. Some of these man-made lichens even look like those that can be found outdoors.

World travelers

The lichens' odd partnership has proved very successful. Lichens grow on every continent and in every part of every continent. On the tops of mountains and in valleys, in the woods and in the desert. On the bark of trees and on the smooth marble of gravestones.

The treeless tundras of the Arctic Circle are covered with Reindeer Moss. Throughout the long winter, this coral-like branching lichen is the chief source of food for reindeers and musk-oxen, and sometimes for hungry men.

An even more famous lichen grows on the rocky slopes of mountains in northern Africa and Asia. Do you remember the Bible story about the children of Israel? After escaping from Egyptian slavery, they wandered in the wilderness for many long years. They were starving until bread rained down from heaven. They called this bread "manna" and they lived on it until they reached the land of Canaan.

The Israelites' manna was probably a lichen. During rain-

REINDEER MOSS

storms, the lichen is washed down from the mountains to the barren plains below. The wind blows it about, heaping it up into mounds several inches thick. It is easy to understand why the Israelites thought that these plants, which appeared so suddenly, had rained down from heaven. Even today plainsmen gather manna-lichen and grind it into flour for bread.

Lichens are found in every country on earth. And perhaps not only on earth. You have listened to discussions about the possibility of life on Mars. When astronomers look at this planet through telescopes they see patches of gray or blue-green, patches that change color at different times of the year. Some astronomers think that *if* there is life on Mars, these patches are lichen.

Practical plants

Although lichens live on a dead-end road, they are useful in many ways. In ancient times they were cooked to make blue and red dyes. Then someone discovered that this coloring could do tricks. A drop of acid, such as lemon juice, turned the blue coloring red. A drop of alkali, such as ammonia, turned the red coloring blue.

If you don't already know this tricky coloring, you will meet it when you study chemistry. Called *litmus*, it is one of the most common tools chemists have for testing the substances with which they work. Litmus is still made from lichens.

Even more important is the lichens' ability to make soil. Yes, to make soil. What do you suppose would happen if you planted a seed on hard, bare rock? If you watered it, it would start to grow. You would see delicate white root hairs and the beginnings of a stem. But soon the roots and stem would shrivel up. A seed can't grow on hard, bare rock. But lichens can.

The tiny threads of the lichen are much, much smaller than the root hairs of a seed plant. Yet they are able to take hold of the rock and dig their way in. Lichens produce a weak acid that slowly dissolves the minerals in rocks. As soon as there is an opening, the threads dig in deeper and deeper. In wet weather they swell with moisture. In dry weather they shrink. This swelling and shrinking helps to enlarge the cracks in the rock.

If you scrape up a patch of lichen, you will see tiny rock

particles, no bigger than grains of sand, on the underside of the plants. The rock itself is no longer smooth. It has been hollowed out until it looks like the surface of a peach pit.

When the lichen dies, the dead plant and the rock particles begin to form soil. After a time there's enough soil to support a moss plant. As the moss continues the job of soil-building, the pocket of earth grows deeper. Ferns move in next, then flowers and grasses. Finally there are trees growing where there was once hard, bare rock.

This soil-building process is not just something that happened a billion years ago. It goes on every day, all around you. Whenever a fire or storm strips an area of its plant life, lichens creep in to repair the damage. That's why they are often called plant pioneers.

The picture on page 49 shows the side of a rock on which lichens and mosses are flourishing and some ferns have already found a foothold. Here and there you will notice straggly bits of grass. The grasses are newcomers now, but in ten years, or twenty, they will crowd out the pioneers.

See for yourself

There are about fifteen thousand different kinds of lichens, many of them growing within a mile or two of your home. Wherever you walk, except along a city street, you can find plants like those in the pictures on pages 43 and 44.

The Parmelia Lichens form a crust on rocks and tree trunks. Some Parmelias are brown, but most are a dull gray-green. Dull gray when the weather is dry, that is, but a sparkling jade-green after a rain or in moist spots in the woods. Can you guess the reason for this color change?

In dry weather, the algae are hidden by the white fungus threads. When the threads fill with moisture they become

LICHENS, MOSSES AND FERNS ON THE SIDE OF A ROCK

transparent. They are like windows through which you can see the green algae. After a storm, lichen-covered rocks glow with color.

The prettiest of all the lichens are the Cladonias. Many of them are so tiny that you have passed them by without noticing them. Once you meet them, you won't forget them, however. The picture on the next page shows the Scarlet-crested Cladonia, whose nickname is "British Soldier." Half an inch tall, its branching wrinkled stalks are silvery. Topping the stalks are bright red knobs—as bright a red as the uniforms worn by British soldiers during the American Revolution. Spores are formed in these scarlet knobs.

SCARLET-CRESTED CLADONIA LICHEN

You may have wondered why we haven't talked before about lichen spores. That's because there is no such thing as a lichen spore.

"But," you interrupt, "spores are formed in those scarlet knobs."

Correct. But they are not lichen spores. They are fungus spores. As soon as they begin to grow they must find algae. Since they can't walk around hunting for partners, they often die of starvation.

As you can see, spores aren't a very safe method of reproduction for lichens. If lichens depended only on spores, they would have become extinct long ago. Like the mosses, they are able to form new plants from broken-off bits of old ones. They also produce thousands of round buds, so small that they look like powder. Each bud is a complete lichen package—an alga wrapped in fungus threads. When the wind blows it away, it is ready to set up housekeeping wherever it lands.

British Soldiers make excellent house plants. You can grow clumps of them in a wine glass or fishbowl. With a little water and even less sunlight, they will live indefinitely.

The bushy Reindeer Moss whose photograph you saw on page 46 is also a Cladonia. It grows in swampy meadows and northern pine forests in our country. Much bigger than the British Soldier, it should be felt as well as seen. If the weather is dry, it is crisp and crunchy. It crackles when you walk on it, the way dry twigs do. On damp days it becomes rubbery, like a sponge.

REINDEER MOSS IN MEASURING GLASS

OLD MAN'S BEARD LICHEN

Reindeer Moss rivals Peat Moss in its ability to absorb water. The measuring glass in the photograph on page 51 holds a clump of Reindeer Moss and six ounces of water. The lichen was dry when it was put in the glass. In an hour, it drank up two ounces—one third—of the water.

YOUNG MAN WEARING OLD MAN'S BEARD

Old Man's Beard is another interesting lichen. Its gray-green streamers dangle from the trees in cool evergreen woods along the seacoast. Although it is draped around live branches, it does no harm to the trees. This is the lichen that is so often confused with Spanish Moss.

There is no need to ask how this plant got its name. The hairy fringe hanging from the branch looks exactly like a beard. You can trim it with a scissors and fasten it to your chin with rubber cement if you want to dress up as Abraham Lincoln or Santa Claus. When your beard gets dry and crumbly, spray water on it to freshen it up!

CHAPTER FOUR

Down in a Valley

The longest dead-end road in the world of flowerless plants is occupied by the fungi. Instead of going forward in one-two-three-four fashion, they seem to have taken a step backward. They have no green coloring matter.

In many ways they are more primitive than the liverworts or the sophisticated mosses. Every cell in their bodies is like every other cell. They have no roots or leaves, no outer protective skin. And, of course, no special place for making or storing food.

Fossil remains of fungi have been found that are nearly two billion years old. Judging by their simple structure, they must have been among the first land plants. Why not the very first? Because they had to follow the green plants. They depend on green plants for food, just as animals do.

The fungi haven't been idle all these millions of years. They have changed and progressed too, in their own special way. Their dead-end road is like a valley, cut into the side of the mountain. There is room in the valley for experiments, but its inhabitants can never climb any higher.

Down in the valley you will see a dazzling display of colors and shapes and sizes and smells. There are five times as many different fungi as there are lichens or mosses, almost ten times as many fungi as there are ferns. Seventy-five thousand fungi is the rough figure that scientists have arrived at.

These plants have many ways of making a living, some of them good from our point of view, some of them bad. The mold that you find on bread is a fungus. So is the baker's yeast that makes bread dough rise.

The smut that destroys ears of corn is a fungus. So is the brewer's yeast that changes corn into alcohol. Athlete's foot comes from a fungus. So does penicillin.

Some fungi make delicious eating. Others contain poisons so powerful that they cause illness or death. You will read more about these poisonous fungi on pages 90-95.

Hunting for fungi is no problem. If you put a piece of moist corn bread in a warm room, it won't take long for mold spores in the air to find their way to the bread and start growing. But the tiny molds—and the yeasts and smuts—are difficult to learn about without a laboratory and microscope. In this chapter, we're going to meet the larger fungi, the plants known as *mushrooms*.

What is a mushroom?

"Well, you buy it in a grocery store and eat it with steak and French fried potatoes."

Right and yet not quite right. You wouldn't say that an apple was an apple tree, would you? The mushroom that you buy is only a part of a plant. It is the short-lived fruiting body, the container for spores.

Look at the picture on the facing page. It shows the main part of the mushroom, the part that lives on year after year. It isn't a root, although its feathery white network of branches looks like a root. It has a special name of its own: *mycelium*.

This mycelium started from a spore. Absorbing food and

moisture, the single cell divided into two. These divided again and again, forming first a long thin chain and finally the tangled threads that you see. They hid from the light, burying themselves in the earth or under the bark of a tree.

The fine white threads cannot make their own food. They must dine on the living and dead matter they find around them —decaying leaves, rotting wood, and sometimes the living tissues of a tree. Without its free lunch, the mycelium would shrivel up and die. You will seldom find mushrooms growing at the seashore. There isn't enough food for them in the sandy soil.

MUSHROOM MYCELIUM

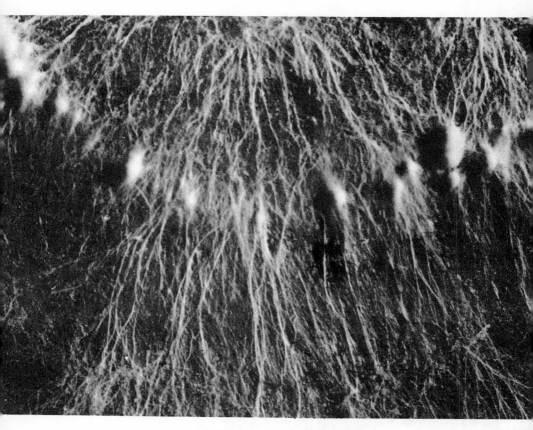

MUSHROOMS BEGINNING TO GROW, BELOW GROUND

The mycelium may live for many months, or even years, without putting in an appearance above ground. When the temperature is just right and there is moisture in the soil, little knots appear on the branching threads. You can see these bumps in the picture on this page. Enlarged in the photograph, they are actually no bigger than pinheads.

Drinking in great quantities of water, they swell like balloons. Although they look soft, they exert a surprising amount of pressure. A clump of growing mushrooms can lift a stone or break through an asphalt sidewalk. Occasionally a cellar floor is laid on top of a buried mycelium. When the mushrooms form they push right through the concrete floor—to the horror of the home owner.

The mushrooms first appear above ground as white blobs the size of marbles. Soon they begin to look like little Humpty Dumpties. Then they are shaped like dumbbells. They are often called *buttons* at this stage.

The outer covering around the buttons begins to split and you can see the beginnings of a cap and stem. The stem grows longer. The cap flattens out. Soon there is a mushroom, fully three inches tall and looking good enough to eat.

Mushrooms grow as fast as Jack's beanstalk. Some kinds reach full size in a single day and dry up and disappear almost as quickly.

The mushrooms in the pictures on these pages are Meadow Mushrooms. Although they grow wild in the fields in summer,

MUSHROOMS APPEARING ABOVE GROUND

MUSHROOM "BUTTON"

MUSHROOM, AFTER OUTER
COVERING HAS SPLIT

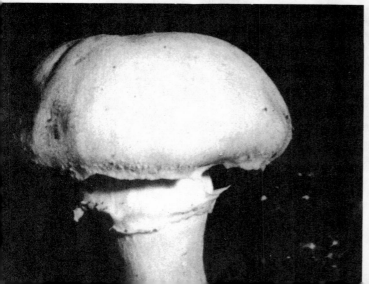

FULL-GROWN
MEADOW MUSHROOM

they are also the grocery-store variety that you eat with steak and French fries. Mushroom farmers raise them for market in caves and special cool dark houses. Their mycelium, which the farmers call *spawn*, is planted in trays and fed on a rich diet of manure.

The cave shown in the photograph on this page contains twenty-four acres of mushrooms in every stage of development. Crews of men spend their days underground here, lighting their way with miners' lamps strapped to their caps as they

MUSHROOM CAVE

tend and gather the growing plants. If there is no mushroom cave or house in your neighborhood, you can find mycelium outdoors, under the bark of a log or in a pile of decaying leaves. You will recognize the fine branching threads as soon as you see them.

An umbrella opens

The Meadow Mushroom is often compared to an umbrella. The handle of the umbrella is the *stem*. The cover is the *cap* and the *gills* of the mushroom are the ribs.

The umbrella starts out closed. When it pushes up from below ground it is wrapped in an outer covering known as a *veil*. As the stem lengthens and the cap unfolds, the veil tears. Part of it remains as a ragged collar around the stem, just below the cap. This is a *ring*. You can see a ring in the photograph of the full-grown Meadow Mushroom and in the picture on the opposite page.

Not all kinds of mushrooms have rings. Often the veil dries up and blows away. Sometimes part of it remains as a *cup* at the base of the stem. Sometimes fragments cling to the cap after it is open. Then they look like loose patches of skin or little warts on the surface of the otherwise smooth cap. The picture on page 63 shows a mushroom cup. If you turn ahead to the photograph of the Fly Mushroom on page 92 you will see a wart-covered cap.

The gills are hidden until the umbrella is wide open. They hang from the underside of the cap, radiating from the stem like the spokes of a wheel. The Meadow Mushroom's gills are pink at first, but they soon turn chocolate brown. Many mushrooms have white gills. Others are black or yellow or even green. It is on these thin colored spokes that the spores are formed.

CUP AT THE BASE OF STEM

When it is full size, the mushroom-umbrella does something no self-respecting umbrella should do. It showers. It rains spores. Billions of them. A single Meadow Mushroom may produce sixteen billion spores.

If an engineer were to design a spore-distributing machine he could scarcely improve on the mushroom-umbrella. The stem lifts the cap above the ground and the spores drop from, the wheel of gills. They fall to the ground or are blown away by the wind. Occasionally a rock or tree root forces the stem to grow sideways instead of upright. What do you suppose happens then?

You can answer the question by looking at the picture on the next page. The stem of the mushroom grew along the ground, unable to dislodge a heavy stone above it. But the upper part

MUSHROOM GILLS

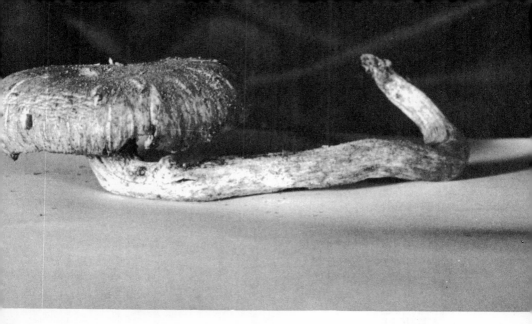

of the stem curved so that the cap was still upright. The cap faces the ground. The gills hang down and the spores can fall free.

You can test this yourself with a mushroom that you find in the woods. (The grocery-store kind won't do.) If you place it on its side, the cap touching a table, its shape will change overnight. The stem will curve upward until the cap is parallel to the table on which it was resting.

Clever thinking on the part of a mushroom? Of course not. The changed position of the cap is a response to the force of gravity. It is the same kind of response that causes the roots of plants to grow downward and their stems upward. Even mushrooms that are not umbrella-shaped—those that grow on the sides of trees, for instance—always have their spore-bearing surface facing the earth.

The mushroom's spores are so small that you can't see one or two or even ten without a microscope. But they are not invisible. You can make them appear by performing a simple trick. Cut off the stem of a fresh, full-grown mushroom. Place the cap, gill-side down, on a piece of paper and cover it with a drinking glass. A few hours later, when you lift up the glass and cap, you will see a design like the one in the picture on this page.

You have made a *spore print*. The white lines show where the gills rested on the paper. The brown rays, which look black in the photograph, are spores. More spores than you could count between now and next Christmas.

MUSHROOM SPORE PRINT

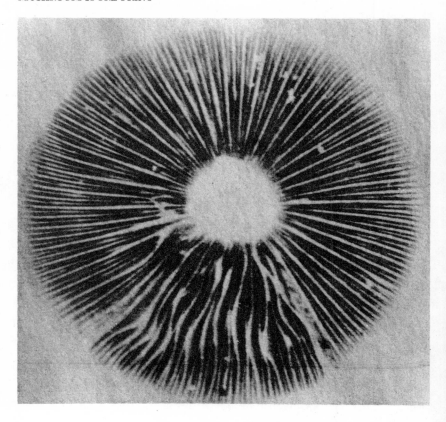

Meadow Mushrooms always have brown spores, while those of the Fly Mushroom are white. Spores may also be black, pink, green, yellow, or rust-colored. If you think your mushroom has light-colored spores, it is better to use black paper for the print.

Spore prints are more than just interesting designs. By making the spores visible, the print helps you to decide what kind of mushroom you have found. But there are many other ways of telling one mushroom from another.

The whole rainbow

When you go on a mushroom hunt, the first thing you think of is color. Most other flowerless plants must stick to chlorophyll green, but fungi have the whole rainbow to choose from. Orange and yellow, pink and red, purple and blue, green, brown, white, jet-black—these are mushroom colors.

On a walk through the woods in summer you can't miss the Orange Chanterelle. It is smaller than many mosses, but its cap and gills and even its stem are a startling orange-red. What color do you suppose the spores are? You're wrong if you guessed orange. All of the Chanterelles have white spores.

You can always recognize these mushrooms by their shape. The cap looks more like a funnel than an umbrella, and the thick branching gills spread down the stem. Some Chanterelles are yellow, others tan or vermilion-red.

The fleshy Russulas are more delicately colored. The satin-smooth cap of the mushroom pictured on page 68 is pink when it is young, fading to a deep red as it grows older. Its stem is white, tinted with red, and its gills are chalk-white.

Do you notice the toothed edge of the cap? This is a clue that will help you to know this mushroom if you see it in the woods. Although *Russula* is the Latin word for red, there are also green, white, and yellow Russulas.

ORANGE CHANTERELLE

RUSSULA

68

Midgets and giants

How big is a mushroom? As small as a thumbtack. As big
as a basketball. The tiny Brownie Cap, whose scientific name is
Galera tenera, is almost hidden from view by blades of grass.
Its slender hollow stem may be three inches long, but its tan
cap seldom measures more than half an inch across. One of the
commonest mushrooms, it grows on lawns and in pastures from
early spring until fall. Doesn't its furrowed cap remind you
of a Chinese peasant hat?

PARASOL MUSHROOMS

Parasol Mushrooms tower over the fragile Brownie Caps. Sometimes their stems are twenty inches long, their caps seven inches wide. The white cap, spotted with freckles, has a brown knob in the center. Its sturdy stem is covered with fine scales. When the parasol is wide open there is a ragged ring below the cap. Such a ring is shown in the photograph on page 63.

70

Cheaper by the dozen

Parasols are found in gardens or alongside the road, growing singly or in pairs. Three is a crowd, they seem to say. The Ink Caps have a different sort of rule: cheaper by the dozen. They always grow in clusters. You will seldom see one of them alone.

The mushrooms in the picture on this page sprang up after a rain, on the stump of a tree that is half-buried in the ground. They are Glistening Ink Caps, so-called because their caps are spotted with shiny scales. Clumps of these mushrooms show up again and again on the same stump, from April-shower time until the first snowfall.

GLISTENING INK CAPS

GLISTENING INK CAPS AFTER A DAY ABOVE GROUND

When the Ink Caps first appear above ground, their egg-shaped caps are tan and their gills are white. A day later the caps have darkened and become torn and ragged-looking. By evening the clump is a moist and shapeless mass, in which only the stems are recognizable. It looks like a perfect picture of decay.

What has happened? As the spores ripen, the gills melt. Instead of remaining firm and white, they dissolve into an ink-like black liquid. The dripping liquid, which has actually been

MANY-CAPPED CLITOCYBES

used for ink, helps to carry away the spores. The mushroom
clump has not decayed. It has gone through a digestive process.

Another mushroom that prefers crowds to a solitary life is
the Many-capped Clitocybe. (*Clitocybe* is a Greek word
meaning "sloping head.") Dozens of mushrooms break
through the ground in the same place. As they grow, their
stems curve outward so that the caps will have room to open.
They pile up, one on top of the other or so close together that
the caps are often pressed into odd shapes. As you can see

73

from the photograph on page 73, they are larger and firmer mushrooms than the Ink Caps. Pale yellow or gray, with a dark area in the center of the caps, their spores are white.

The Many-capped Clitocybes crowd together the way people do when they are watching a parade. Other mushrooms grow side by side, forming circles as if for a game of dodge ball. There are many old stories about these rings of mushrooms.

People used to think that they were charmed circles where fairies danced on moonlit nights. Or that they marked the spot where goblin bands had buried treasure. Or that the devil, breathing fire and brimstone, held ghostly court there. Even today, they are still called *fairy rings*. Can you figure out the scientific explanation for their presence?

FAIRY RING

The mycelium of some kinds of mushrooms lives on year after year. As it grows, two things happen. Its web of threads spreads outward. It dies at its center when it has used up all the available food there. Each year the fine white threads spread farther from the center.

The mushrooms that appear in the grass mark the growth of the underground mycelium. Each year their ring grows larger. In some parts of the country there are fairy rings eight hundred feet wide. They started to grow long before Columbus discovered America.

The fairy ring on the opposite page is made by small, tan-capped mushrooms known as Fairy-ring Mushrooms or Scotch Bonnets. They look something like Brownie Caps. Although more than a dozen common mushrooms form rings, these are the best known. You will find them springing up late in summer and in the fall. A golf course is a particularly good place to hunt for fairy rings.

It's the shape that counts

Not all mushrooms look like umbrellas. Many kinds that grow on trees or fallen logs have no stems at all or have stubby stems attached to the edge of their caps. Oyster Mushrooms grow in clusters on living and dead wood, never on the ground. Their fleshy caps are fan-shaped. Often pure white, with white gills and spores, they are a striking sight in the woods in summer and fall. They taste as good as they look, with a flavor something like oysters. In some countries, they are cultivated for food. Perhaps one day you will try Oyster Mushroom stew.

Here's a riddle for you. When is a shelf not a shelf?

Answer: When it's a mushroom.

The mushrooms pictured on page 77 and 78 are called *Shelf Fungi* because of the way their caps stick out from the wood

OYSTER MUSHROOMS

on which they grow. Another name for them is *Bracket Fungi*.

Birch Polypores are little white balls when they break through the bark of the tree. As they get bigger, the caps flatten and grow darker. They are tough and corky, not soft like Oyster Mushrooms. If you look closely at the picture you can see that these mushroom-shelves tear the birch bark as they grow. Dozens of Birch Polypores are scattered over the surface of a single tree or birch log.

Scaly Polypores usually grow in clusters from thick short stems. Their overlapping caps may measure a foot across.

BIRCH POLYPORES

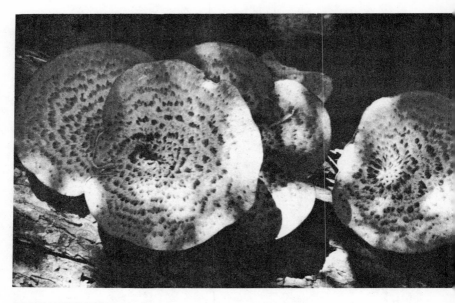

SCALY POLYPORES

COMMON SHELF FUNGI

Tawny yellow with brown scales, they shrivel and turn black in winter.

The Common Shelf Fungus feels like wood. It grows bigger each year, its growth marked by a series of rings on the surface of its cap. Some of these shelves are four or five years old.

The smooth white underside of the shelf offers a fine surface for drawing pictures. When it is scratched with the point of a pencil or knife, it turns dark brown. Even after the mushroom dries, the markings remain. If you use a shelf fungus for outdoor sketching, remember to draw your picture carefully. Once you've started, you can't erase!

No gills at all

Not all mushrooms have gills. When you look at the underside of a shelf fungus you will notice that it consists of thousands of little holes. Each hole is the mouth of a hollow tube. The spores develop inside these tubes, dropping out through the holes when they are ripe. The holes are known as *pores,* which explains *polypore,* a Greek word meaning "many pores."

There are other pore mushrooms in addition to the woody shelves. The untidy-looking mushroom in the picture on page 80 is the Pine Cone Mushroom. You will always know it by its tufted blackish cap and rough stem. The same size as a Meadow Mushroom, it is also fleshy and umbrella-shaped. Not until you look at the underside of its cap do you realize that it is related to the shelf fungi.

The photographs on page 81 show the honeycomb of pores and a spore print made by the Pine Cone Mushroom. The mouths of the tubes are white when young, but they darken as they grow older or when they are touched. The spores are dark brown. If you compare this spore print with the gill mushroom's you will see how different the two patterns are.

PINE CONE MUSHROOM

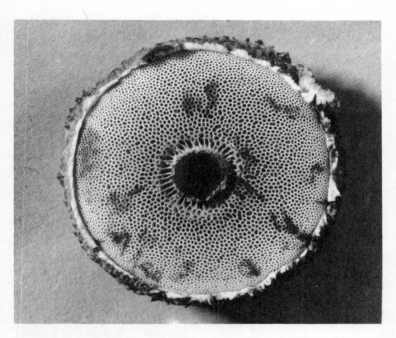

PORES OF PINE CONE MUSHROOM

SPORE PRINT, PINE CONE MUSHROOM

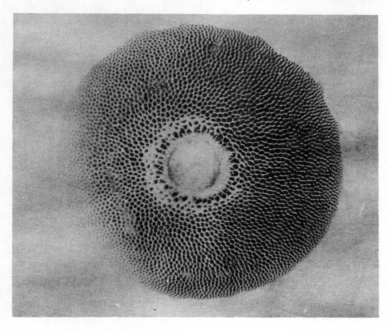

TWO-COLORED BOLETUS

The Two-colored Boletus is another pore mushroom. When you meet it in the woods, its cap and stem are wine-colored and its tubes a bright yellow. As it ages, yellow spots appear on the surface of the cap and the tubes turn blue if they are bruised. "Three-colored" would really be a better name for it. Other Boletus mushrooms have scarlet caps and orange or green tubes.

More exceptions

Not all mushrooms are umbrella-shaped. Or have gills. Or pores. Some develop spores on small, fleshy teeth, others on upright branches. One of the best-known mushrooms showers spores from the surface of its cap. Other familiar kinds are shaped like cups or balls.

The Coral Mushroom reminds you of coral reefs under the sea, but the plant corals are soft and delicate and they droop in bright sunlight. Their spores are formed on the cluster of upright branches. The plant in the photograph is pale yellow but other Coral Mushrooms are red or have red-tipped branches.

CORAL MUSHROOM

MORELS

Morels would never win a prize for beauty. They have fat, flesh-colored stems and caps that look like bits of an old rubber sponge. Their spores develop in the wrinkles and ridges of the cone-shaped caps.

But the Morels are a reminder that beauty is only skin-deep. Of all the mushrooms pictured in this book, they are considered

the best-tasting. Because they often appear on burned-over ground, people in the West used to burn down whole forests in order to encourage their growth!

No one would start a forest fire today for the sake of a mushroom dinner, but Morels are still a favorite food. If you visit a park or woods near a big city in April or May, you're likely to see stoop-shouldered men and women brushing aside piles of dead leaves or peering at the ground under a tree. They're prospecting for Morels, not uranium.

Another group of odd-shaped mushrooms are the Cup Fungi. They grow on the ground or on rotting wood. Although their cups look empty, spores form on the surface of the cups and pop out when ripe. Some Cup Fungi are round and leathery. Others form clusters of ruffled fleshy cups which may be three or four inches broad.

The Puffballs break all rules. No cap or stem, no gills or pores, no branches or cups. Yet these balls, which are nicknamed "Smokeballs" or "Devil's Snuffboxes," start out in the

PASTURE PUFFBALL

same way that gill mushrooms do. Little buttons when they push above ground, they simply increase in size until they are as round as balloons.

The flesh of a young Puffball is white and firm. The inside of the ball soon becomes soft and brown. When full grown, it is nothing but a dusty mass of threads and spores. An unbelievable number of spores. More than you could count in your entire lifetime.

When the spores are ripe, irregular cracks appear on the outside of the ball. Inside, the tiny threads twist and turn until they have forced the spores out through the cracks. The outer covering dries up and disappears as the spores are scattered.

PUFFBALL "EXPLOSION"

REMAINS OF PUFFBALL AFTER "EXPLOSION"

Doubtless you have heard of the mushroom-shaped cloud that follows an atom-bomb explosion. You can make your own mushroom cloud by gently tapping a ripe Puffball. The "smoke" that you see in the picture is really a cloud of microscopic spores. When the cloud blows away, all that is left are fragments of thread and crumbly bits of the mushroom's outer skin. The ground is covered with purple-brown spores. Some Puffballs have a short thick base which remains in the ground, marking the spot of the "explosion."

The Pasture Puffball shown in these pictures is bigger than a baseball. Although it is the largest of the common Puffballs you would scarcely notice it alongside a Giant Puffball. A really big Giant may measure six feet around and weigh more than twenty pounds. It contains enough mushroom "meat" to feed a good-sized family. In the days before matches were invented the threads inside these balls were used as tinder.

The Gem-studded Puffball is a tiny relative of the Pasture Puffball. It grows in clusters on the ground, seldom more than two inches high. White, studded with soft white spines, it turns brown as it grows old. The ripe spores puff out through an opening on the top of the mushroom. When you squeeze these Puffballs they spurt smoke, as if they were miniature volcanoes.

GEM-STUDDED PUFFBALLS

Danger, beware!

While many mushrooms are good to eat, a few kinds are poisonous. Not just a little poisonous either, but really deadly poisonous.

The Emperor Nero, the same Nero who fiddled while Rome burned, once murdered all of the guests at his banquet table by serving them poisonous mushrooms. Even today, hundreds of people die each year because they have eaten one of the killer varieties. A single bite of some mushrooms may cause serious illness.

Perhaps you have heard people say, "You can eat mushrooms, but not toadstools." Or, "If you can peel the skin from a mushroom cap, it is safe to eat." Or, "If a silver spoon turns black when it is cooked with mushrooms, the mushrooms are poisonous."

There isn't a word of truth in any of these sayings. "Toadstool" is just a nickname for mushroom. When someone calls a mushroom a toadstool, he usually means that it is unpleasant to look at. But some of the ugliest mushrooms make good eating while some of the handsomest are poisonous.

There is no easy way to tell the man-killers from the edible plants. They don't have a skull and crossbones stamped on them as the poisonous drugs in your medicine cabinet do. The only way to know whether or not a mushroom is poisonous is to *know* it. To know exactly what it looks like so that you can always recognize it. To be as sure of its appearance as you are of your own face when you look in a mirror.

Hair curly or straight? Brown eyes or blue? Freckles? Dimples? Square chin? There are corresponding questions that can be asked about mushrooms.

The picture on the next page shows a young Fly Mushroom.

YOUNG FLY MUSHROOM

It looks very much like the Meadow Mushroom button, doesn't it? But the cap of the Meadow Mushroom is smooth, that of the Fly Mushroom is rough.

Now study the pictures of the full-grown Fly Mushroom on pages 92 and 93. Its cap is bright red or orange, fading to yellow as it ripens. The surface of the cap is dotted with white warts. It has a ring around its stem and a flattened cup at its base. Its gills and spores are white. It grows singly, never in clumps.

Look at the Fly Mushroom, but never, never eat it! Although it is far prettier than the Meadow Mushroom, it is one of the most poisonous common mushrooms.

To recognize the Fly Mushroom when you meet it in the woods, you must ask questions. What color are the cap, the gills, the spores? Does it have warts, a ring, a cup? Does it grow alone or in a clump? When the answers add up, you will *know* you have found a Fly Mushroom. There is no short cut to this knowledge.

FLY MUSHROOM

The scientific name of the Fly Mushroom is *Amanita Muscaria*. Since most—but not all—of the Amanitas are poisonous, it is worth learning about them. Their cap and gill colors vary, but they always have white spores and a ring and cup. If you

FLY MUSHROOM, SIDE VIEW

turn back to page 63, you will see a baglike cup, much like
that of the Destroying Angel, deadliest of all the Amanitas.
These cups are known as *death cups* because they are found
on many poisonous mushrooms.

There are other poisonous mushrooms in addition to the Amanitas. Some of the attractive Russulas may not kill you but they can make you uncomfortably sick. So can several of the Boletus mushrooms.

Even mushrooms which are safe to eat should be picked only when the plants are in good condition. Puffballs are edible when their flesh is firm and white but no one would want to taste them after their spores form. Nor would you eat an Ink Cap if its gills had begun to melt.

There is one basic rule to remember if you gather mushrooms. Don't eat them unless you are sure you *know* all about them. Never take a bite to see if they taste good!

Tree-killers

Woody shelf fungi are not poisonous, but they can do more damage than the deadly Amanitas. Sometimes their spores land on a live tree and make their way inside through a hole in the bark. The growing mycelium feeds on the tree, digesting the wood until it becomes soft and crumbly. Foresters call these tree-killers *punks* because they change the solid wood of the tree into a powdery mass.

The only sure way to stop this mushroom invasion is by prevention, by sealing up holes in the bark before the spores have a chance to enter. Once the mycelium has gained a foothold —a thread-hold—it is difficult to root out. Then it's time to call the tree surgeon and arrange for an operation.

The picture on the opposite page shows a cluster of Scaly Polypores growing from a wound in an elm tree. Each summer the owner of the tree breaks off the curving shelves, only to find that they reappear the following year. The shelves themselves are not doing the damage. They will wither anyway after they have shed their spores. The mycelium from which they

SCALY POLYPORES ON AN ELM TREE

grow is the enemy. Its fine white threads are spreading through the living tissue and heartwood of the tree.

There is a war going on between the elm tree and the mushroom. The mushroom is slowly eating the tree. It will take a long time, but eventually the mushroom is sure to win. Even after the big tree dies, the conquering mushroom will live on.

CHAPTER FIVE

Some Dwarf Giants

You are back on the main road again, following the sign that says, "This way to the top of the mountain." Here are plants that have progressed in one-two-three-four fashion. They have real roots, not just slender anchoring threads. They have stems with special tubes for carrying water and food to the different parts of the plants. Their stalks and their narrow needle-thin leaves have thick coverings to slow down the evaporation of water.

These are the *horsetails* and *club mosses*. Horsetails have nothing to do with horses, or club mosses with mosses. Relatives of the ferns, they are known as *fern allies*.

Most flowerless plants have remained close to the ground. Not so with the horsetails and club mosses. They shot up into the air, growing sixty feet, eighty feet, one hundred feet tall.

"But that makes them trees," you protest. "A horsetail tree? A club moss tree? Even the names sound silly."

Yes, a horsetail tree sixty feet tall. A club moss tree a hundred feet tall. And not in the mountains of Tibet or the Amazon jungle either. There are horsetails along the railroad tracks in your town and club mosses in the woods.

You still don't believe it?

Have you ever known someone who was the descendant of a famous person? He doesn't look impressive and his own life isn't exciting, but he can tell wonderful stories about his great-

great-great-grandma who cooked the Pilgrims' first Thanksgiving turkey or his great-grandpa who was a conductor on the Underground Railroad in slavery days. He can show you the bed in which his ancestor slept or the quill pen he used when he wrote a famous speech.

That's the way it is with horsetails and club mosses. They are plants with a grand and glorious past. They are the descendants of the giant trees of the Coal Age forests. They look exactly like their ancestors. Except. Except that instead of being sixty feet tall, they are now six feet or six inches tall. They are dwarf copies of their former giant selves.

Do you remember when, from the window of the time machine, you saw trees with jointed trunks and frills of leaves growing from each joint? Those were horsetails. Do you remember the trees with flat overlapping green leaves that covered trunks and branches? Those were club mosses.

At that time they were among the largest plants on earth. Their spores covered the waters of the ancient swamps. Their decaying bodies were gradually compressed into coal.

Like the dinosaurs, they became too big for their own good. They never developed the strong wood of an oak tree or the seed-plant's ability to withstand great changes in climate. When the mountains rose, when the swamps dried out, when great white sheets of ice spread from the poles, new kinds of plant life appeared. Some of the trees in the coal forests died, leaving only fossil records behind them. The horsetails and club mosses shrank in size, to become living fossils. When you see them today, it is as if you were looking at them through the wrong end of a telescope.

Horsetails

Early in the spring, near the railroad tracks or along a road where the soil is poor, watch for clumps of flesh-colored plants.

FIELD HORSETAILS, SPORE-BEARING STALKS

The Field Horsetail, pushing up through the gravel and cinders, is as much a sign of spring as the first robin or violet.

It grows from an underground stem, producing two different-looking stalks each season. The pale plants in the photograph on page 99 grow rapidly—two inches a day—until they are close to a foot high. Their jointed stems are hollow, with the sections fitting neatly together like pieces of pipe. If you pull a stem apart at the joints, you will hear a "pop" as the air inside is released.

FOOD-MAKING STALKS OF FIELD HORSETAILS PUSH ABOVE GROUND

The flat black teeth that surround each joint are remnants of leaves, useless for food-making. Nourishment comes from stored-up food in the underground stem. These stalks have only one job—to produce spores. The yellow cones at their tips contain thousands of tiny green spores. As soon as they are ripe, the stalks wither. By summer there is no sign of them.

Even before the spore-bearers have disappeared, the horse-tails' food-making stalks push above ground. You can see their odd-shaped beginnings in the picture on page 100. When full

FIELD HORSETAILS: FULL GROWN FOOD-MAKING STALKS

SHINING CLUB MOSS

grown, they are bushy plants with a circle of narrow green branches growing from each joint. Do the brushlike branches look to you like horses' tails? This imagined resemblance has given them their name.

Another familiar horsetail is the Scouring Rush. Its spore-bearing cone grows at the tip of a green, unbranched stem. These stems, sometimes six feet tall, contain silica, one of the elements in sand paper and household cleansers. In colonial times, the gritty stems of the Scouring Rush were used for cleaning pots and pans. You will find them handy on an overnight camping trip.

Club mosses

Horsetails have learned to live in sand and gravel, but club mosses need the rich soil of the woods. These descendants of once-proud trees have become creeping plants with trailing or underground stems. The Shining Club Moss is one of the most common members of the group. It grows in clusters, its stiff stalks covered with shiny, pointed, green leaves.

GROUND CEDAR

The spore cases of the Shining Club Moss are formed at the base of the leaves. On other club mosses, the spores grow on separate stalks, in erect cones that look like miniature pine cones. You can see these in the photograph of the Ground Cedar on page 103. The flat overlapping leaves of this plant resemble the needles of cedar trees.

The Ground Pine is the tallest of the club mosses. Its trailing stem is buried deep in the soil and its new shoots grow singly instead of in clumps. Late in the summer, cone-shaped spore

GROUND PINES

cases form among the topmost branches of the plants. Although they are only a few inches high, Ground Pines look exactly like trees. If you kneel down beside them, it is easy to imagine that you are back in the days of the ancient coal forests.

Despite their grand beginnings, the graceful club mosses face an inglorious end. They have been uprooted so recklessly for Christmas wreaths and winter table decorations that they are hard to find in some parts of the country. One day you may have to visit a museum instead of a forest to see these living fossils.

CHAPTER SIX

This Way to the Top!

As you climb the mountain, ferns are the last stopover before daisies and oak trees. Their leaves are bigger than the club mosses'. Their stems are sturdier than the horsetails' and their roots are tougher. One-two-three-four-five.

In the swampy forests of the Coal Age there were ferns fifty feet tall, with woody trunks and broad green leaves. Alongside the tree ferns were plants that looked like ferns. But they had seeds growing on the surface of their leaves. Some of the seeds were tiny, others as big as ping-pong balls.

These were *seed ferns*. They died out before the days of the dinosaurs, but their fossil remains show the link between ferns and flowering plants.

Not so very long ago, people were sure that ferns had flowers. They had roots and stems and leaves, didn't they? Therefore, they *must* have flowers and seeds. Just because you had never seen a fern flower didn't mean that it couldn't exist. It meant only that you hadn't searched enough, in the right places and at the right time. And perhaps you hadn't used the right magic word.

All sorts of stories were told about ferns. They had tiny blue flowers that bloomed on only one night of the year. At the stroke of midnight on Midsummer's Eve, these flowers ripened and their shining seed fell to the ground. If you could catch this seed on a white cloth, you would possess magical powers.

A pinch of fern seed on your shoes made you invisible. You could travel anywhere in the world and no one would be able to see you. Fern seed gave you second sight. You could look into the past and the future. You could find lost things. You knew where to dig for buried treasure.

People really believed these stories about the "wondrous one-night-seeding fern." On Midsummer's Eve, groups of men went to the woods, equipped with white cloths and sorcerers' charms. If they failed to find fern seed, it was because their charms were wrong!

"Watching the fern" was so popular—and so closely associated with witchcraft—that churchmen in France finally forbade such expeditions.

The legends surrounding ferns aren't as silly as they sound. As is the case of many other ancient tales, they were an attempt to explain something for which there was as yet no scientific explanation.

Watching the fern

Nowadays you can "watch the fern" on any summer day. Only you will use a magnifying glass instead of magic words if you want to see fern "seed."

As you have no doubt guessed, the "seeds" that the fern watchers were looking for were really spores. The picture on page 108 shows hundreds of them scattered across a piece of white paper. Dustlike dots, each is no more than one five-hundredth of an inch in size.

Perhaps you would like to plant some of these spores. You can scoop them up on the tip of a pocketknife and shake them over a dish of water or dampened soil. But no matter how carefully you take care of them, they won't grow into familiar-looking ferns.

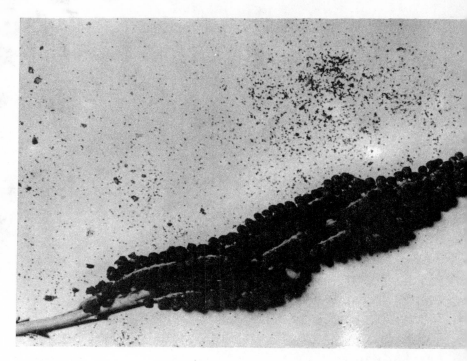

FERN SPORES

Another riddle. When is a fern not a fern?
When it's a *prothallus*.

Ferns, along with most flowerless plants, lead a double life. Do you remember the mosses' alternation of generations? "Parents and children never look alike. Grandparents and grandchildren always do." The same rule holds true for ferns.

A fern spore grows into a prothallus, a green heart-shaped plant much like a liverwort. The photograph of the prothallus on page 109 is greatly enlarged. In real life it is no bigger than your thumbnail and so thin that you can almost see through it.

On the underside of the prothallus there are egg cells and sperms. The ripe sperms swim to the eggs and fertilize them. Again that word *swim*. Even the ferns remind you of their watery past. Their sperms need raindrops or dew in which to travel.

Still attached to the prothallus, the fertilized egg develops slowly. Weeks or even months later, it sends a tiny root down into the earth and a leaf toward the sun. The first leaves of the new plant bear little resemblance to the fern-to-be. They take their food from the prothallus until they are strong enough to manufacture their own. Then the prothallus dries up and disappears.

FERN'S FIRST LEAVES

PROTHALLUS

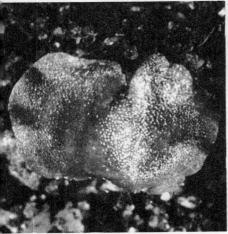

The photograph below shows a six-month-old fern plant. The withered remains of the prothallus can still be seen, but the fern at last looks like a fern. The second generation has taken over.

SIX-MONTH-OLD FERN

The fern looks like a fern

But what does a fern look like? There is no simple answer to this question. In the tropical rain forests of South America, and in Australia and the Pacific Islands, there are tree ferns which are even bigger than their Coal Age ancestors.

In our country the sturdy Bracken takes over fields and hillsides, growing six feet tall in sunlight and poor soil. The fragile Wall Rue hides away, burying its roots in rock crevices and lifting its leaves only a few inches above its moss neighbors.

BRACKEN FERNS

WALL RUE FERN

The Boston Fern, which covers the trunks of palm trees in the Florida Everglades, is equally at home in a flowerpot in your living room.

There are 250 different kinds of ferns in the United States. Their roots and stems are different. Their buds are different. Their leaves are different. Their spore cases are different.

112

BOSTON FERN

Take roots and stems, for instance

Tree ferns have tall upright trunks. Their roots are at the bottom of the trunk and their leaves grow from the top. Just the kind of thing you expect from a plant. But most ferns don't grow this way.

Those near your home have horizontal stems which grow under the ground. These buried, sideways-growing stems are known as *rootstocks*.

113

Some rootstocks are slender and branching. They spread for many feet underground. The photograph on this page shows the woody rootstock of the Marsh Fern. The fine black hairs are roots. The upright stems are the stalks of the leaves which grow singly or in pairs along the branches.

Other rootstocks are short and thick. Their leaves are produced in clumps. The Cinnamon Fern rootstock creeps along the surface of the ground, sending out wiry roots from all sides. Each spring new leaves appear at one end of the rootstock, while the other end dies. The remains of old roots and leaves add to its bulk and its shaggy appearance. Some Cinnamon Fern rootstocks are more than a hundred years old. On flat, swampy ground they stand out like little islands.

ROOTSTOCK, MARSH FERN

114

ROOTSTOCK, CINNAMON FERN

Buds

There are always clusters of buds at the base of fern leaves—buds for this year, buds for next year and the year after. If one crop of leaves is destroyed, another can quickly take its place. Like the Boy Scouts, the ferns' motto is "Be Prepared."

The bud of a fern is a tight little package, protected against cold and dampness by wooly or paper-like scales. Each part of

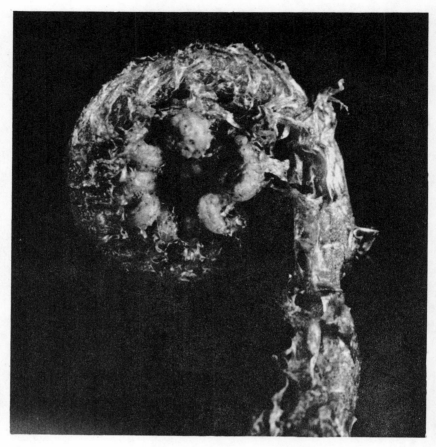

FERN FIDDLEHEAD

the leaf-to-be is rolled in on itself, with the tip in the center of the spiral. As it pushes above ground, it slowly uncoils. If you have ever taken the mainspring out of an old clock and watched it unwind, you will have some idea of the mechanism of the fern bud.

These graceful spirals are known as *fiddleheads,* because they resemble the curving head of a violin. Of course, it would be more correct to say that the head of the violin resembles a fern bud. The ferns came first, remember!

116

RATTLESNAKE FERN LEAVES UNFOLDING

No other plant bud is constructed in quite this way. Whenever you see a fiddlehead, you can be sure that you have found a fern. The opposite is not always true, however. There are a few ferns that don't start out as fiddleheads. The leaf parts of the Rattlesnake Fern are folded rather than coiled. They open out flat, like the pages of a book.

Every fern fiddlehead has a personality of its own. Before the leaves are out on the trees in spring, the buds of the Cinnamon Fern appear above ground. At first the fiddleheads are

CINNAMON FERN FIDDLEHEADS

CINNAMON FERN FIDDLEHEADS,
CLOSE-UP

completely covered with white wool. They are the plumpest,
the wooliest, the whitest of all fern buds. But they don't stay
that way for long. The wooly coats become rust-colored and
fall off, leaving only loose tufts of wool at the base of the
leaves.

Pushing upward quickly, they grow an inch or more each

CINNAMON FERN FIDDLEHEADS UNCOILING

day. Long before the stalk has reached full size, the leaves begin to unfurl. You can follow their growth in the photographs on these pages. In the first pictures the fiddleheads are only two or three inches above their black rootstocks. In the last they are three feet tall and there is still more to come.

Christmas Fern fiddleheads lean backward and curve and twist as if they were dancing. Even when the leaflets along the stem are open, the tip of the leaf is still a tightly coiled spiral. These slender fiddleheads seem to be covered with silk rather than wool. The thin scales soon turn brown, but early in the spring they are silver-colored.

CHRISTMAS FERN FIDDLEHEADS

Bracken buds grow singly, with new buds appearing throughout the summer. Sometimes a fiddlehead begins to uncoil before it has pushed above ground, so that it is shaped at first like a croquet hoop. The hoop quickly turns into a hook. Then the thick, red-brown stem straightens out.

The picture on this page shows a Bracken fiddlehead when its stem is two feet tall. The parts of the leaf are still rolled up. As the bud opens, it divides into three balls which, in turn, divide into three more and then three more again. Because some people think that the balls resemble the claws of a big bird, the Bracken has been nicknamed "Eagle Fern."

BRACKEN FERN FIDDLEHEAD, CLOSE UP

BRACKEN FIDDLEHEAD

BRACKEN FIDDLEHEAD WHEN STEM IS TWO FEET LONG

SENSITIVE FERN FIDDLEHEADS

In contrast to the coarse, hairy Bracken, the little Sensitive Fern fiddleheads are smooth and shiny. The uncoiling spirals and partly opened leaves are often wine-red. As the plant grows, the rich color fades to green.

Fiddleheads are not only good to look at. Some of them are also good to eat. When the Bracken buds are small, they can be cooked and eaten like asparagus, while Ostrich Fern fiddleheads and young leaves taste like spinach.

Leaves

How would you describe a fern leaf?

"Feathery," you say. "Graceful, delicate, green."

Like the leaves in the picture on this page. Each has a single midrib with finely cut leaflets branching off from it. Like a feather. In fact, like a fern.

But if you think that all fern leaves are "fernlike," you are in for a surprise. All of them start with a stalk that grows from the rootstock. All of them have a single midrib. They are all more or less green. And there the resemblance ends.

BOULDER FERN LEAVES

Fern leaves are so different in shape that you need a special list of words to describe them. A few ferns have *simple* leaves. Instead of being feathery, they are all in one piece, without any divisions. The Walking Fern, whose photograph appears on page 147, has simple leaves. So have the Adder's-tongue and the Hart's-tongue.

It's hard to think of the fleshy leaf of the Adder's-tongue as a fern. The long stalk with the pointed tip is the spore-bearing part of the leaf. Does this spike make you think of the tongue of a snake? People used to boil Adder's-tongue leaves to make a medicine for snake bites.

ADDER'S-TONGUE FERN

HART'S-TONGUE FERN

The Hart's-tongue's ruffled leaves are thick and leathery. It is one of the rarest American ferns, growing wild only in a few spots in New York, Michigan, and Tennessee. In England where it is common, its leaves are often two feet long. Sometimes this plant is called Seaweed Fern.

Some ferns have *lobed* leaves. The leaf is divided, but the divisions do not reach all the way to the midrib. The Sensitive Fern and the Polypody are examples of lobed leaves.

The Common Polypody is found in most parts of the country, growing on rocks in shady places. A close relative, the Gray Polypody, often forms clumps on tree trunks and branches. The thick little leaves stay green all winter.

There are Sensitive Ferns wherever the ground is damp, in woods or open fields, and at the edge of streams. By midsummer, the broad leaves look anything but "sensitive." Probably they acquired their name because they wither with the first frosts in fall.

COMMON POLYPODY FERN

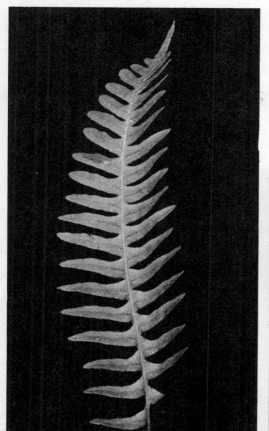

SENSITIVE FERN

Most fern leaves are divided into leaflets. These leaflets are known as *pinnae*. A leaf with only a single set of leaflets is *once-pinnate*. Although the ferns pictured on this page and and the next three pages are quite different in appearance, they are all once-pinnate.

The Deer Fern grows along the West Coast from Washington to California. Its shiny, polished leaves resemble those of the eastern Christmas Fern, whose picture appears on page 154.

DEER FERN

BEECH FERN

Beech Ferns grow in shady spots in the woods. Their triangular leaves are light green. Do you notice how the lowest pair of pinnae poke forward? This is a clue that will help you to recognize Beech Ferns.

Both the Cinnamon and Ostrich Ferns are big. They grow in vaselike clumps, their curving leaves often six feet tall. You can easily tell them apart by looking at the outlines of their

128

NEW YORK
FERN

leaves. The broad Ostrich leaf narrows at its base. Its lowest pinnae are only a fraction of the size of those in the middle of the leaf.

The New York Fern also has tiny pinnae at the base of its leaf, but you could never mistake it for the Ostrich Fern. Seldom more than eighteen inches high, it is a thin delicate fern, yellow-green in color. In spite of its name, it is found in all of the eastern states, and as far west as Arkansas and Minnesota.

LADY FERN

There are ferns whose leaflets are again divided into leaflets. These leaves are *twice-pinnate*. The Lady Fern is a good example of this kind of leaf. Like the Beech Fern, its bottom pinnae usually poke forward.

PURPLE CLIFFBRAKE FERN

The Purple Cliffbrake is a puzzler. The lower part of its leaf is twice-pinnate and the upper part once-pinnate. And that's not all. Sometimes the leaf shape varies and you find small leaves that are twice-pinnate and larger ones in the same clump with only one set of leaflets. The one thing that doesn't change is their color. The leathery leaflets are a bright blue-green and the wiry stalks are purple.

131

Now look at this picture of the Maidenhair Fern. At last you're coming to a leaf that is really "fernlike." Although it is twice-pinnate, it seems better to describe it as circular. Its midrib divides into two and curves to form half-circles. The feathery pinnae are pale green, the stalk and midrib a shiny jet-black.

The strangest of the twice-pinnate leaves is that of the Climbing Fern. It grows like a vine, its stalk and midrib twisting around any support they can find. It is so light and slender that it can even climb on blades of grass.

MAIDENHAIR FERN

The lobed pinnae are shaped like the palm of your hand, with from five to seven fingers. In the United States, Climbing Fern leaves are three or four feet long, but in tropical countries some varieties climb fifty feet, twisting around the trunks of trees.

CLIMBING FERN

Climbing Ferns once grew along the Atlantic coast from New Hampshire to Florida and inland as far west as Ohio. Now their decorative leaves are hard to find outside of fern gardens. Their scarcity can't be blamed on earthquakes or glaciers or on anything but people. As long ago as 1869, the Connecticut legislature passed a law protecting Climbing Ferns.

The stiff glossy Bracken leaf is triangular in outline. The broad lower branches are three-times pinnate. The middle branches are twice-pinnate. The upper part of the leaf is once-pinnate and the tip is lobed. Remember this is not a tree you are looking at, but a single fern leaf!

Often called Brake, it is one of the few plants that people all over the world are familiar with. Three or four feet tall in most localities, it sometimes reaches a height of fifteen feet. It grows in the Maine woods and along the beach in Florida, on the midwestern plains and the slopes of the Rocky Mountains. And on the English moors and the Swiss Alps and the islands off the coast of India. In some countries the roofs of houses are thatched with Bracken leaves. In others, they are used as bedding for cattle.

There are more legends about Bracken than about any other fern. The Brake gave protection against goblins and witches. If you cut its stalk you would see the initial of your sweetheart. If you burned its leaves, you would have rain. An English king who wanted sunny weather while he was visiting in the provinces forbade the burning of the Brake during his vacation. And of course it was on the Bracken leaf that the mystic fern seed ripened.

BRACKEN FERN

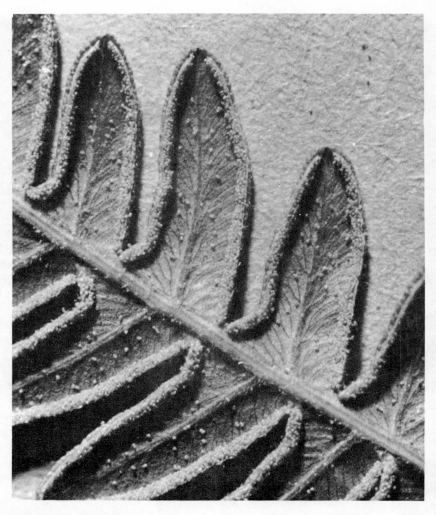

BRACKEN FRUIT DOTS

Certainly no one would believe any of these stories today. But try "watching" this fern late in summer. On the back of its leaf you will see a narrow border, outlining the edges of the pinnae. The border is made up of thousands of little round balls. They are greatly enlarged in the photograph on this page.

136

Strange fruit

The tiny globes, which *do* look like seeds, are spore cases. Each one contains from forty-eight to sixty-four spores. The scientific name for these groups of spore cases is *sori* (singular, *sorus*), but they are usually spoken of as *fruit dots.*

Every fern has its own distinctive fruit-dot pattern. You can

CHRISTMAS FERN FRUIT DOTS

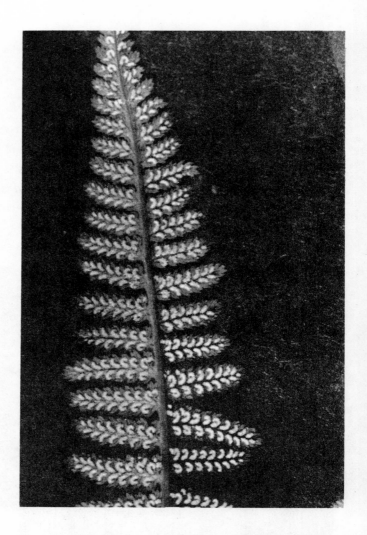

LADY FERN
FRUIT DOTS

be sure of the names of many common ferns by noticing the shape of the fruit dots.

Compare the pictures on pages 136, 137, and on these pages. The Bracken's fruit dots form a neat line around the edge of the leaflets, while those of the Christmas Fern spread all over the underside. The curving fruit dots of the Lady Fern grow in double rows. Horseshoe-shaped and a silvery white when they are young, they darken and straighten out as they ripen.

POLYPODY FRUIT DOTS

EVERGREEN WOOD FERN FRUIT DOTS

The big brown fruit dots of the Polypody look like freckles, the Wood Ferns' dots like curled-up caterpillars. On the leaves of the Evergreen Wood Fern, the "caterpillars" grow close to the central vein of the leaflet. On the Marginal Wood Fern, they are always at the edge. "Marginal" refers to the fact that the fruits dots are located on the margin of the leaf. The Wood Ferns, which are also called Shield Ferns, are the ferns that florists use in bouquets and for banquet-table decorations. The leaves are collected in the summer and stored in refrigerators.

140

MARGINAL WOOD FERN FRUIT DOTS

Not all ferns have fruit dots on the backs of their leaves. Sometimes part of a leaf is given over to spore cases. Sometimes there are separate spore-bearing leaves which bear little resemblance to the other leaves of the plant.

Along a country road or in a damp meadow early in the spring you are almost sure to see Interrupted Ferns.

"Interrupted by what?" you may wonder.

By the fruit dots, of course. Each clump has two kinds of leaves, green ones which look much like those of the Cinnamon Fern and startling two-colored leaves, part green and part chocolate-brown.

INTERRUPTED FERN

INTERRUPTED FERN,
FERTILE LEAF

As you can see in the close-up picture, the lower and upper pinnae are ordinary leaflets, but the middle ones consist entirely of fruit dots. After the spores are ripe, these pinnae drop off. The spore-bearing leaves are *fertile*. Those which do not produce spores are *sterile*.

ROYAL FERNS

The fertile leaves of the Royal Fern arrange matters differently. Here the base of the leaf remains green while the spores grow in a flowerlike spike at the tip. The Royal is often called Flowering Fern.

The Cinnamon Fern goes even further in its division of labor. Its fertile leaves are stiff cinnamon-colored clubs on separate

CINNAMON FERN,
FERTILE LEAF

GRAPE FERN

stalks. In the fiddlehead picture on page 118 you can see them uncoiling. The close-up on this page shows the lacy design of the fruit dots. If you touch them when they are ripe, clouds of bright green spores puff out.

Some fertile leaves resemble berries or rows of beads on a string. You can see the beadlike fruit dots of the Grape Fern on this page, those of the Sensitive Fern on pages 108 and 122.

145

Most spores are scattered as soon as they are ripe, but the spore cases of the Sensitive Fern remain sealed all winter and its spores are not released until the following spring.

Look, Ma, no spores!

If all of the billions of fern spores survived, what would the world be like? Ferns would blanket the earth and crowd out other plants. Instead of oak trees and daisies you would only see fern leaves. You would be back in the days of the coal forests.

But the world has changed since those days. Only a tiny fraction of the spores floating in the air ever land in the damp shady places they must find in order to grow. An even smaller fraction survive the long process of spore-to-prothallus-to-fertile-fern-leaf.

Because spores and the water-loving prothalli are really not very efficient, many ferns have developed other methods of reproduction. The Bracken produces new plants all along its branching rootstock, which may be twenty feet long. Buried deep under the ground, the woody rootstock is protected against dryness and cold weather. Even if all the spores on earth were destroyed, there would still be thickets of Bracken.

Have you ever seen a Walking Fern walk? Their narrow triangular leaves arch over until they touch the ground. Roots grow from the tip of the triangle and a new plant is formed. Soon the new plant develops tapering leaves that "walk." Before long, the parent is surrounded by its children and grandchildren—all of them produced without spores.

In the picture on the facing page you can recognize a parent plant and half a dozen of its babies. Walking Ferns are not found in all parts of the country. They grow best on limestone rocks, in the deep shade of the woods.

WALKING FERNS

BULB-BEARING BLADDER FERN, UNDERSIDE OF LEAF

The Bulb-bearing Bladder Fern has an even safer way of reproducing itself. On the underside of its leaf there are bulbs as well as fruit dots. Each fleshy bulb is about half as big as a pea. When it is ripe, it falls to the ground and immediately sprouts roots and leaves. This fern helps you to imagine what the ancient seed ferns looked like.

Home, sweet home

You can live almost anywhere—in the city or the country, in a skyscraper or farmhouse, or even a tent in summer. But most ferns can't change their homes. A woods fern will die if the trees that shelter it are cut down. A fern that grows alongside a stream can't move to a dry meadow. A fern from the mountains shuns the valley.

If you know the homes that different ferns prefer you will know where to hunt for them. You won't look for Bracken in shady forests because this tough fern with its deeply buried rootstock likes the wide-open spaces. You will go to swamps or damp meadows for Cinnamon Ferns, to rich woods for the Maidenhair, to the banks of a stream for the Ostrich Fern.

Sometimes the name of a fern tells you its address. It's not hard to guess where the Marsh Fern lives. It grows best in low, wet places, or bordering a pond where water lilies bloom. Never in the water, but just at its edge, so that its roots can cling to the soft, wet mud. When Marsh Ferns are established in the right kind of home their slender yellow-green leaves, set on long, stiff stalks, grow close together until they have crowded out neighboring plants.

There's a whole group of ferns that won't live—can't live—without rocks. Some of them make their homes at the base of a boulder. Others prefer its top, or the cracks and crevices on the side of a cliff. Still others demand stony soil in which to spread their roots.

MARSH FERNS

BOULDER FERNS

Sometimes any kind of rock will do. Sometimes it must be limestone. The Purple Cliffbrake and the tiny Wall Rue, for instance, insist on limestone. There's no use hunting for them outside of limestone regions. Can you figure out the reason for this?

The Boulder Fern is another fern whose name gives you its exact address: rocky fields and hillsides. Look for boulders and you will find Boulder Ferns. In the stony pastures of New England almost every rock outcropping is bordered by clumps of these finely cut pale leaves. Even when you see them at a distance as you ride by in a car, you cannot fail to recognize them.

Besides a permanent address, Boulder Ferns have a distinctive odor. When their leaves are crushed or drying, they give off a strong, sweet smell. For this reason, they are often called Hay-scented Ferns. Everyone likes these pretty, fragrant leaves except the farmer. His cows refuse to eat them, and their creeping rootstocks are difficult to dig out of his pasture.

While the Boulder Fern lives at the bottom of a rock, the Common Polypody makes itself at home on top. These small, leathery-leaved ferns perch on moss-covered boulders or flat rock ledges, spreading rapidly in the thin dry soil. You will seldom see them growing on the ground.

COMMON POLYPODY FERN

They follow the lichens and mosses as soil pioneers. Their branching rootstocks keep the earth from blowing away and their dead, decaying leaves add to its bulk, until there is enough soil to support larger plants. The name "Polypody," coming from the Greek, means "many feet." When you see a tangled mat of ferns covering a rock you can be sure you have found the many feet of the Common Polypody.

Perhaps the fussiest home hunter of all the rock ferns is the Maidenhair Spleenwort. It finds its home not at the bottom, not at the top, but in tiny cracks on the face of a boulder. And if the rock is covered with moss, so much the better.

While its roots take firm hold in the crevices, its narrow leaves spray out in decorative rosettes. Found throughout the country, it is the smallest of the common ferns, although it is

MAIDENHAIR SPLEENWORT FERNS

CHRISTMAS FERNS

inches larger than the Wall Rue. It is often transplanted to rock gardens, where it feels at home in the chinks of a stone wall.

Christmas Ferns grow on the ground, but they prefer stony soil and shade. Although their name doesn't tell you their address, it tells something else about these plants. Along with their close relatives, the Sword Ferns of the West, they stay fresh and green all year round. At Christmas time, you can brush aside the snow to find their glossy leaves. If you pick the leaves carefully, without disrupting the rootstock or next year's well-wrapped buds, you won't harm the plants.

Next stop, seeds and flowers

It has taken a long time to climb the mountain. There are paths you haven't explored, and side roads that you may want to visit again. But most of the pieces of the jigsaw puzzle are spread out in front of you.

In the days of the giant ferns and horsetails, there were other trees in the coal forest. Some had special leaves which were different from the ordinary leaves of the tree. They were small and overlapping, and they lacked green coloring matter. They were like the cones you see on pine trees.

When a spore ripened on one of these leaves, it didn't fall to the ground to form a prothallus. Instead, it remained on the leaf. It developed into a baby plant while it was still a part of the parent.

These baby plants were *seeds*.

As the years rolled by, there were improvements in the special seed-leaves. Some of the leaves formed hollow boxes to enclose the plant-to-be. Others became brightly colored petals.

These clusters of seed-leaves were *flowers*.

But that is another story.

Index

The numbers in italics indicate pages on which pictures appear.

About the Author

DOROTHY STERLING is a native New Yorker who lives now in Rye, New York, with her husband and children, and spends her summers on Cape Cod. She was educated at Wellesley and Barnard Colleges and worked at Time, Inc., before leaving to devote herself to her family and her writing. Not only is Mrs. Sterling a good writer, but she is also a painstaking and thorough researcher with a long list of fiction, mysteries, and scientific books to her credit.